A Special Gift

For:

_____

From:

_____

Date:

_____

ISBN: 1-57051-031-8

COVER/INTERIOR:
KOECHEL PETERSON & ASSOCIATES

PRINTED IN SINGAPORE

A Little Cup of Tea

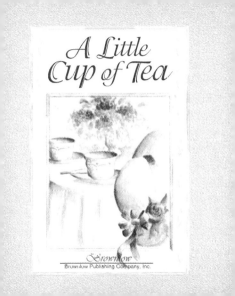

Brownlow
Brownlow Publishing Company, Inc.

Little Treasures Miniature Books

A Little Cup of Tea

All Things Great & Small

Angels of Friendship

Baby's First Little Bible

Cherished Bible Stories

Dear Teacher

Faith

For My Secret Pal

From Friend to Friend

Grandmothers Are for Loving

Hope

Love

Mother

My Sister, My Friend

Precious Are the Promises

Quilted Hearts

Soft as the Voice of an Angel

The Night the Angels Sang

Sincere Friendship

Friendship!
how I love the feeling,
Sweetly soothing
to the mind,
When o'er my soul
sweet mem'ry stealing,
Leaves a holy calm behind.

ANONYMOUS

What bring joy to the heart
is not so much the friend's gift
as the friend's love.

ST. AELRED OF RIEVAULX

Friendship is a strong
and habitual inclination in
two persons to promote the good
and happiness of one another.

EUSTACE BUDGELL

The Book of Tea

The first Book of Tea was written by Lu Yu (A.D. 733-804) after five years of hermithood and research. The detailed compendium made him a revered celebrity in China.

My Friend

You're my friend—

What a thing friendship is,
world without end!
How it gives the heart
and soul a stir-up!

ROBERT BROWNING

There is a great deal of
poetry and fine sentiment
in a chest of tea.

RALPH WALDO EMERSON

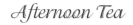

Afternoon Tea

$\mathcal{A}$nna, the seventh Duchess of Bedford, began the institution known as "Afternoon Tea" in England during the 1840's. She commonly had a "sinking feeling" in the late afternoon because the customary lunch was

only a few snacks
and dinner was not served
until eight o'clock.
So she began taking
tea and cakes at
five o'clock and inviting
a few friends.

There's a special kind
of freedom friends enjoy.
Freedom to share
innermost thoughts,
to ask a favor, to
show their true feeling.
The freedom simply
to be themselves.

The Best Friend

The best friend is an atmosphere
Warm with all
inspirations dear,
Wherein we breathe the large,
free breath
Of life that hath
no taint of death.

Our friend is

an unconscious part

of every

True beat of our heart;

A strength, a growth, whence

we derive

Feelings that keep

the world alive.

ANONYMOUS

Though Love
be deeper,
Friendship is more wide.

CORINNE ROOSEVELT ROBINSON

We have been friends together
in sunshine and shade.

CAROLINE NORTON

Russian Tea

The first tea reached Russia in 1618. By 1796, Russians were consuming over 6000 camel loads of tea per year. Most Russians ate one large meal daily and sipped glasses of tea the rest of the day. Every home had a samovar and the tea was always hot and strong.

When the heart
overflows with gratitude,
or with any other sweet
and sacred sentiment,
what is the word
to which it would
give utterance?
A friend.

WALTER SAVAGE LANDOR

What lies behind us, and what
lies before us are tiny matters,
compared to what lies within us.

RALPH WALDO EMERSON

Everyone must have felt that
a cheerful friend is like
a sunny day, which sheds
its brightness on all around.

LORD AVEBURY

A Little Cup of Tea

If you are cold,
tea will warm you—
If you are heated,
it will cool you—
If you are depressed,
it will cheer you—
If you are excited,
it will calm you.

WILLIAM E. GLADSTONE

We can fall down by ourselves,
but it takes a friendly hand
to lift us up.

Maturity is the stage of life
when you don't see eye to eye
but can walk arm in arm.

All the Tea in China

A shortened phrase
first used in Australia
in the 1890's that meant
not at any price,
"not for all
the tea in China."

There's something
so beautiful in coming
on one's very own
inmost thoughts in another.
In one way it's
one of the greatest
pleasures one has.

OLIVE SCHREINER

There are few hours in life more agreeable than the hour dedicated to the ceremony known as afternoon tea.

HENRY JAMES

The true atmosphere
of friendship is a sunny one.
Griefs and disappointments
do not thrive in its clear,
healthy light.

RANDOLPH BOURNE

If life were predictable
it would cease to be life
and be without flavor.

ELEANOR ROOSEVELT

It is best to be
with those in time
we hope to be
with in eternity.

SIR THOMAS FULLER

Tea and Longevity

In China, long ago, tea was an ingredient in immortality potions. Even today, some maintain that tea drinking helps one to live to a ripe old age.

It is hard to believe
that anything is
worthwhile, unless...
what is infinitely
precious to us is
precious alike
to another mind.

GEORGE ELIOT

Bread

Be gentle when
you touch bread.
Let it not lie uncared for
and unwanted. So often
bread is taken for granted.
There is so much
beauty in bread:
beauty of sun and soil,

beauty of patient toil.
Winds and rains
have caressed it,
Christ often blessed it.
Be gentle when
you touch bread.

ANONYMOUS

Let us be first to give a
friendly sign, to nod first,
smile first, speak first
and if such a thing is
necessary— forgive first.

ANONYMOUS

The true test of friendship
is to be able to sit or walk
with a friend for an hour
in perfect silence
without wearying of
one another's company.

DINAH MARIA MULOCK CRAIK

$Friendship$—

pure unselfish friendship,

all through life's allotted

span, nurtures, strengthens,

widens, lengthens, man's

relationship with man.

UNKNOWN

The best
cure for an empty
day or a longing heart is to
find people who need you.
Look, the world is
full of them.

ANONYMOUS

*T*hank God for tea!
What would the
world do without tea?—
How did it exist?
I am glad I was
not born before tea.

SYDNEY SMITH, BRITISH EVANGELIST

Separate from the pleasure
of your company,
I don't much care if I never
see a mountain in my life.

CHARLES LAMB

*T*reat your friends like family
and your family like friends.

ANONYMOUS

*W*hat joy is better
than the news
of friends?

ROBERT BROWNING

Old Friendships

Full of tears and warm
is an old friendship
That asks no longer
deeds of gallantry,
Or any deed at all —
save that the friend shall be
Alive and breathing somewhere,
like a song.

EUNICE TIETIENS

A friend is the gift of God,
and he only who made hearts
can unite them.

SOUTHBY

Like everything breathing of
kindness —
Like these is the
love of a friend.

A. P. STANLEY

The First English Tea Room

While more than 500 coffeehouses existed in London in the late 17th century, by 1717 Thomas Twining had opened the first gathering house strictly for tea.

Women were also
now welcome and tea
soon became
the most popular
non-alcoholic beverage
in England.

*E*very one
that flatters thee
Is no friend in misery.
Words are easy,
like the wind;
Faithful friends
are hard to find.

RICHARD BARNFIELD

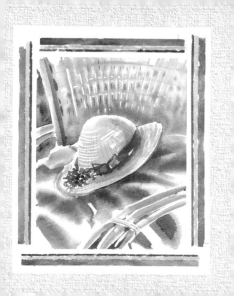

Drinking a daily cup of tea
Will surely starve
the apothec'ry.

CHINESE PROVERB

Forget Me Not

But oh! if grief thy steps attend,
If want, if sickness be thy lot,
And thou require
a soothing friend,
Forget me not,
forget me not.

AMELIA OPIE

The one who knows how to
show and to accept kindness
will be a friend
better than any possession.
SOPHOCLES

Friendship is neither a formality
nor a mode: it is rather a life.
DAVID GRAYSON

In friendship we find
nothing false or insincere;
everything is
straightforward,
and springs
from the heart.

CICERO

Confessions of
a Tea Drinker

I am a hardened and
shameless tea drinker,
who has for many years
diluted his meals with
only the infusion of
this fascinating plant;
whose kettle has

scarcely time to cool;
who with tea amuses
the evening, with tea
solaces the midnight,
and with tea welcomes
the morning.

SAMUEL JOHNSON

I hold this task to be
the highest task for a bond
between two people;
that each protects
the solitude
of the other.

RAINER MARIA RILKE

I avoid looking forward
or backward, and try to
keep looking upward.

CHARLOTTE BRONTË

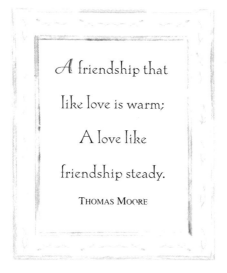

A friendship that

like love is warm;

A love like

friendship steady.

THOMAS MOORE

We can only have the highest happiness by having wide thoughts, and much feeling for the rest of the world, as well as ourselves.

GEORGE ELIOT

God has put something noble and good into every heart His hand created.

MARK TWAIN

Home and found my wife making of tea; a drink Mr. Pelling, the potticary, tells her is good for her cold and defluxions.

SAMUEL PEPYS, DIARY, 1667

A clay pot sitting in the sun will always be a clay pot. It has to go through the white heat of the furnace to become porcelain.

MILDRED WITTE STOUVEN

*T*herefore encourage one another and build each other up, just as in fact you are doing.

1 THESSALONIANS 5:11

Some Other Name

Oh, call it by some better name,
For friendship sounds too cold.

THOMAS MOORE

The person who
sows seeds of kindness
will have a perpetual harvest.

ANONYMOUS

You can win
more friends with
your ears
than your mouth.

ANONYMOUS

Look here, if this is coffee,
I want tea; but if this is tea,
then I wish for coffee.

PUNCH

A Tea Party

You see, merry Phillis,
that dear little maid,
Has invited Belinda to tea;
Her nice little garden
is shaded by trees,—
What pleasanter place
could there be?
There's a cake full of plums,

there are strawberries too,
And the table is set
on the green;
I'm fond of a carpet
all daisies and grass,—
Could a prettier picture be seen?

KATE GREENAWAY

A Friend Indeed

He that is thy friend indeed,
He will help thee in thy need:
If thou sorrow, he will weep;
If thou wake, he cannot sleep;
Thus of every grief in heart
He with thee doth bear a part.
These are certain signs to show
Faithful friend from faltering foe.

RICHARD BARNFIELD

*B*etter to be deprived
of food for three days
than of tea for one.

CHINESE PROVERB

The Tea Bag

In 1908, New York tea importer Thomas Sullivan sent out samples of different kinds of tea, each of which had been sewn into little, individual silk bags. Some customers mistakenly made tea with the little packages. Soon many people were complaining when the tea was not in the tiny pouches, and the tea bag was invented.

Let our lives be
pure as snow-fields,
where our footsteps leave
a mark but not a stain.

MADAME SWETCHINE

It is surely better
to pardon too much
than to condemn too much.

GEORGE ELIOT

Into My Garden

Here is a little forest,
Whose leaf is ever green;
Here is a brighter garden,
Where not a frost has been;
In its unfading flowers
I hear the bright bee hum;
Prithee, my brother,
Into my garden come!

EMILY DICKINSON

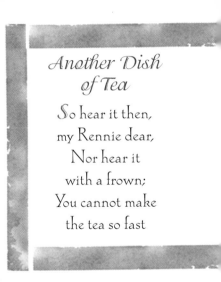

Another Dish
of Tea

So hear it then,
my Rennie dear,
Nor hear it
with a frown;
You cannot make
the tea so fast

As I can gulp it down.
I therefore pray thee,
Rennie dear,
That thou wilt
give to me
With cream and sugar
softened well,
Another dish of tea!

Dr. Samuel Johnson

Small service is
true service while it lasts.
Of humblest friends, bright
creature scorn not one!
The daisy, by the shadow
that it casts,
Protects the lingering
dew-drop from
the sun.

WORDSWORTH

Let friend trust friend,
and love demand love's like.

ROBERT BROWNING

If we would build on a sure
foundation in friendship,
we must love our friends
for their sakes rather than
for our own; we must
look at their truth
to themselves full as much
as their truth to us.

CHARLOTTE BRONTË

I count myself
in nothing else so happy,
As in a soul rememb'ring
my good friends.

WILLIAM SHAKESPEARE

*W*hen friends stop being frank
and useful to each other,
the whole world loses
some of its radiance.

ANATOLE BROYARD

A Recipe for Friends

One recipe for friendship is the right mixture of commonality and difference. You've got to have enough in common so that you understand each other and enough difference so that there is something to exchange.

ROBERT WEISS

I know not whether our names
will be immortal;
I am sure our friendship will.

WALTER SAVAGE LANDOR

There is essential meanness
in the wish to get the better
of any one. The only
competition worthy of a
wise woman is with herself.

MRS. JAMESON

Here thou,
great Anna!
whom three realms obey,
Dost sometimes
counsel take—
and sometimes tea.

ALEXANDER POPE

I think those happiest who
find their happiness early,
but I do not see why
happiness should be rejected
because it is the will
of Providence that it
should not be found till late.

DINAH MARIA MULOCK CRAIK

The thing that counts most
in pursuit of happiness
is choosing the right
traveling companion.

ANONYMOUS

If you want enemies,
excel others;
if you want friends,
let others excel you.

CHARLES CALEB COLTON

The hot water is to
remain upon it (the tea)
no longer than while
you can say the
Miserere Psalm (Psalm 51)
very leisurely.

SIR KENELM DIGBY

While there's tea, there's hope.

SIR ARTHUR PINERO

My best friend is the
one who brings out
the best in me.

HENRY FORD

We secure our friends
not by accepting favors
but by doing them.

THUCYDIDES

Give thy heart's best
treasure, and the more
thou spendest from
thy little store, with a
double bounty, God
will give thee more.

ADELAIDE A. PROCTER

More Tea than England

America's love of tea began
before the British arrived.
In 1674, when New Amsterdam
became New York under
British rule, the colony
probably drank more tea
than all of England.

Half the wrongs people do to us
are through sheer ignorance.
We must be patient.
In your patience
possess ye your souls.

DINAH MARIA MULOCK CRAIK

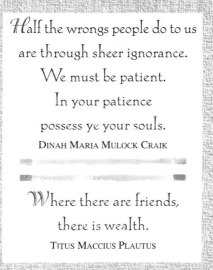

Where there are friends,
there is wealth.

TITUS MACCIUS PLAUTUS

A Precious Jewel

We are the weakest of spendthrifts if we let one friend drop off through inattention, or let one push away another, or if we hold aloof from one for petty jealousy, or heedless roughness.

Would you throw away a diamond because it pricked you?

One good friend is not to
be weighed against all the
jewels of the earth.

UNKNOWN

Quiet Moments With a Friend